Invertebrates

Octopuses, Squids, and Their Relatives

Cephalopods

Beth Blaxland
for the Australian Museum

CHELSEA HOUSE
PUBLISHERS
A Haights Cross Communications Company
Philadelphia

Chelsea House Publishers
1974 Sproul Road, Suite 400
Broomall, PA 19008-0914

The Chelsea House world wide web address is www.chelseahouse.com

Library of Congress Cataloging-in-Publication Data Applied for.
ISBN 0-7910-6992-3

First published in 2002 by
MACMILLAN EDUCATION AUSTRALIA PTY LTD
627 Chapel St, South Yarra, Australia, 3141

Edited by Anna Fern
Text design by Polar Design Pty Ltd
Cover design by Polar Design Pty Ltd
Illustrations by Peter Mather, Watershed Art and Design
Australian Museum Publishing Unit: Jenny Saunders and Kate Lowe
Australian Museum Series Editor: Deborah White
Australian Museum Scientific Adviser: Ian Loch

Printed in China

Acknowledgements
Cover photograph: Northern blue-ringed octopus, courtesy of Clay Bryce/Lochman Transparencies.

Alex Steffe/Lochman Transparencies, pp. 5, 7 (top), 30; Carl Miller-Bios/Auscape, p. 8 (top); Clay Bryce/Lochman Transparencies, pp. 6, 8 (bottom), 13 (bottom), 14 (bottom), 16, 23 (all), 24–5 (middle), 29 (bottom); D. Parer & E. Parer-Cook/Auscape, pp. 20, 28–9; David B. Fleetham – OSF/Auscape, pp. 6 (top), 15; Eva Boogaard/Lochman Transparencies, pp. 12 (top), 26–7 (middle); Geoff Taylor/Lochman Transparencies, p. 10; Fred Bavendam – Peter Arnold/Auscape, p. 4; Jeffery L. Rotman – Peter Arnold/ Auscape, p. 6 (bottom); Karen Gowlett-Holmes/Nature Focus, pp. 9 (top), 11, 12, (bottom), 13 (top), 18, 19 (bottom), 21 (all), 24 (top), 25 (top), 27; Kevin Deacon/ Auscape, pp. 7 (bottom), 14 (top); Mark Spencer/Auscape, p. 19 (top); Peter & Margy Nicholas/Lochman Transparencies, p. 22.

Contents

Glossary words
When a word is printed in **bold**, you can look up its meaning in the Glossary on page 31.

What are cephalopods?

Cephalopods are a group of invertebrate animals. An invertebrate is an animal that does not have a backbone. There are many different kinds of invertebrates. Some other examples of invertebrates are crabs, insects and centipedes. Many other animals are invertebrates too. Can you think of any?

There are four main kinds of cephalopods and all of them live in the sea. The main kinds of cephalopods are:

◎ octopuses
◎ squids
◎ cuttlefishes
◎ nautiluses.

How do you say it?

centipedes:	*sent-i-peeds*
cephalopods:	*sef-al-o-pods*
invertebrate:	*in-vert-a-bret*
mantle:	*man-tl*
mollusks:	*mol-usks*
nautiluses:	*naw-tuh-lis-es*

Did you know

A cuttlefish is a kind of cephalopod, but a cuttlefish is not a fish. Fish are very different from cephalopods. A cephalopod is an invertebrate – it has no backbone. A fish has a skeleton with a backbone.

▽ **An octopus is a cephalopod.**

mantle

arms

tube-shaped funnel

General features of cephalopods

Cephalopods' closest relatives are invertebrates such as snails and slugs. Snails, slugs and cephalopods all belong to a big group of invertebrates called **mollusks**.

All mollusks, including cephalopods, have the same general features. Mollusks are invertebrates that:

◎ have a soft body

◎ have a **mantle**, which is the special part of their skin that often grows a shell

◎ move about using a strong muscle under their body. Most mollusks crawl about on a flat muscle called a **foot**. Some mollusks swim using a tube-shaped muscle called a **funnel**.

Cephalopods are a little different from other kinds of mollusks, such as snails and slugs. Cephalopods are the only mollusks that have:

◎ a thick mantle that covers most of their body

◎ a funnel under their body

◎ a circle of strong arms and long **tentacles** around their mouth.

⚊ **A cuttlefish is a cephalopod. All cephalopods have a thick mantle, a strong tube-shaped muscle called a funnel and many arms or tentacles surrounding their mouth.**

Fascinating fact

Cephalopods are one group of mollusks. There are about 100,000 different types of mollusks, but only about 650 different types of cephalopods.

Cephalopod bodies

A cephalopod's soft body has a head, a **visceral mass** and a funnel. The visceral mass contains the stomach and other body organs. It is covered by a special kind of skin called the mantle. The head has two large eyes and a mouth with short, hard jaws that look like a bird's beak. Cephalopods have a circle of arms and tentacles around their mouths. Many cephalopods also have a shell, but the shell is often buried inside the mantle.

The bodies of octopuses, squids, cuttlefishes and nautiluses are each a little different.

Octopuses

An octopus has a rounded body with eight strong arms. Most octopuses have suckers on their arms. Octopuses do not have a shell.

Squids

A squid has a long, narrow body. A short flap of skin called a fin lies on each side of the mantle. Squids have eight arms and two long tentacles. They have suckers on the insides of their arms and on the ends of their tentacles. Some squids also have hooks or claws on their tentacles. Squids have a very thin, flat shell under their mantle.

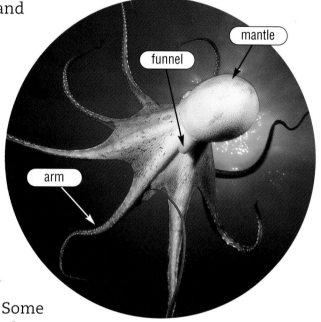

mantle
funnel
arm

This is an octopus.

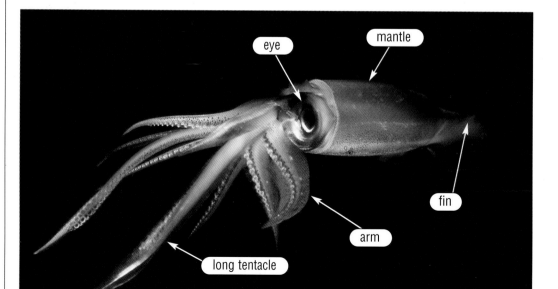

eye
mantle
fin
arm
long tentacle

This is a squid.

Cuttlefishes

A cuttlefish has a short, wide body with a fin along each side of the mantle. Cuttlefishes have eight arms and two long tentacles. There are suckers on the insides of their arms and on the ends of their tentacles. A cuttlefish has a shell hidden inside its mantle.

Did you know ❓

Suckers help squids, octopuses and cuttlefishes to catch and hold their food.

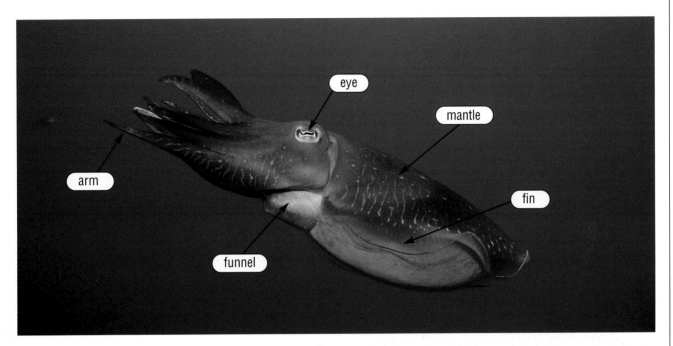

⋀ **This cuttlefish's arms are stretched out, but its two long tentacles are tucked away.**

Nautiluses

A nautilus has a large shell around its body. The shell can be closed with a thick flap of skin called a hood. A nautilus does not have arms, but it does have about 90 thin tentacles that it can stretch out of its shell. These tentacles do not have suckers.

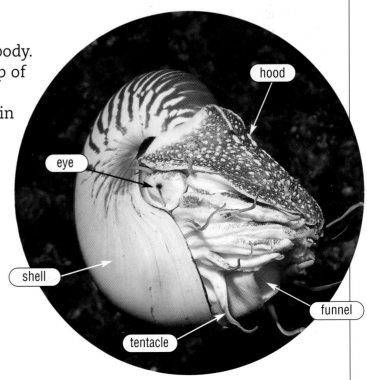

⊗ **This nautilus has pulled in most of its tentacles.**

How do you say it?

visceral mass: *viss*-er-al mass

Special features of cephalopod bodies

Funnel

The funnel is a tube-shaped muscle that helps a cephalopod swim. First the cephalopod sucks water in through holes between its head and mantle. Then it squirts a jet of water out of its funnel to push its body through the water. The cephalopod points its funnel in different directions to swim forward, backwards or sideways. For example, it swims backwards by pointing its funnel forward.

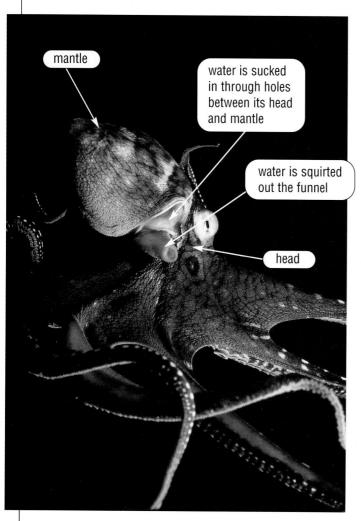

mantle

water is sucked in through holes between its head and mantle

water is squirted out the funnel

head

◁ **A cephalopod uses its funnel to swim.**

Shell

A cephalopod's shell grows from its mantle. The shell grows bigger as the body grows. Nautiluses grow a large shell around their bodies. Squids and cuttlefishes grow a small shell inside their bodies. A squid's shell is long and very thin like a feather. A cuttlefish has a thicker shell that looks a little like a surfboard. These small shells make it easier for squids and cuttlefishes to swim quickly. A nautilus can only swim slowly because its large shell slows it down.

 Each one of these shells was once inside a cuttlefish's body.

Did you know ❓

A cuttlefish's shell is called a cuttlebone. When cuttlefishes die, their soft bodies are eaten or rot away, and only their hard cuttlebones are left behind. These cuttlebones often wash up onto beaches.

Arms and tentacles

Most cephalopods have arms that are thick and strong, with suckers all along one side. Octopuses, squids and cuttlefishes all have eight arms.

Most cephalopods also have tentacles. Tentacles are long and thin, with either a few suckers at the ends or no suckers at all. Squids, cuttlefishes and nautiluses all have tentacles. Squids and cuttlefishes have two tentacles that are about twice as long as their arms. They tuck their tentacles into pockets near their mouths when they are not feeding. Nautiluses have many shorter tentacles that they can tuck away inside their shells.

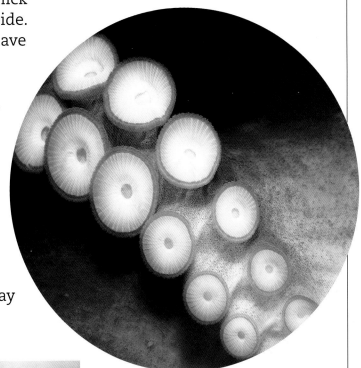

⋀ **This octopus arm has two rows of suckers.**

arm

tentacle

◔ **Squids and cuttlefishes have eight arms and two long tentacles.**

Changing color

Many cephalopods can quickly change their body color to attract a mate, hide or scare away enemies. Some cephalopods can make their skin turn lighter or darker. Others can make different-colored patterns on their bodies. They can turn yellow, orange, brown, red, blue, black or a mixture of these colors. Sometimes they keep flashing different colors and patterns across their bodies.

The life cycle of cephalopods

Male cephalopods often have special ways to introduce themselves to a female. Some males change the color of their skin. Some males hold up their arms or tentacles in special ways. This attracts the females to the males.

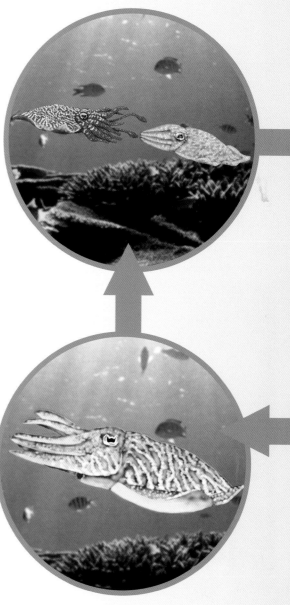

Cephalopods make new cephalopods through sexual reproduction. The female provides eggs and the male provides **sperm**. When an egg and a sperm join, a new cephalopod begins to grow.

△ **Two young pin-stripe squids have just hatched from this group of eggs on the sea floor.**

When the young cephalopods hatch from their eggs, they look like tiny adults. Some young cephalopods stay on the sea floor but others drift around in the sea for a while. Most young octopuses, squids and cuttlefishes mature into adults when they are between five months and 2 years old. Nautiluses mature when they are 5 to 10 years old. The adult cephalopods are then ready to reproduce.

To **reproduce**, the adult male provides sperm. The male uses one of his arms to take a bundle of sperm from his body and put it in the female's body.

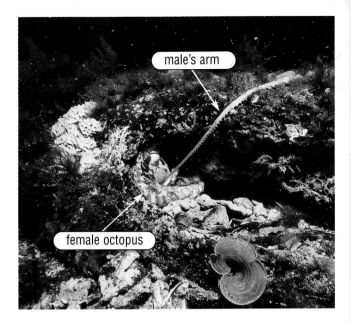

male's arm

female octopus

⚠ **In this picture, a male octopus is hiding behind a rock while he tries to place his sperm inside a female's body. He is hiding in case the bigger female decides to attack him.**

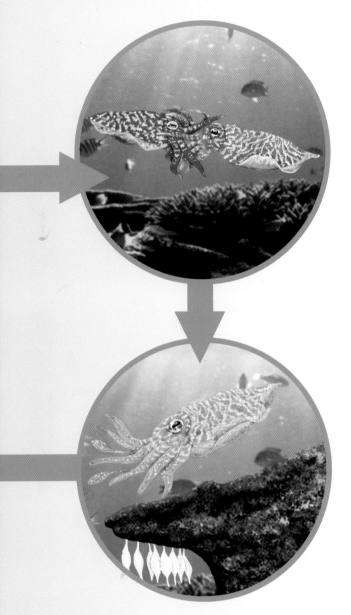

Fascinating fact

Some small squids live for only three months, but nautiluses can live for as long as 20 years. Cephalopods that live in very deep, cold water tend to live longer than cephalopods that live in shallow, warm water.

Did you know ❓

Most octopuses, squids and cuttlefishes reproduce once and then die. Nautiluses can reproduce for many years.

When an egg and sperm join, a young cephalopod begins to grow inside the egg. Most female octopuses, cuttlefishes, nautiluses and squids attach their eggs to the sea floor. Some squids just release their eggs into the sea water. Octopuses are different from other cephalopods because the females look after their eggs until they hatch. Most adult cephalopods only mate once, then die soon after the eggs are laid.

Where cephalopods live

Cephalopods live in seas all around the world. They can be found everywhere, from the deepest parts of the sea to the seashore. Many cephalopods live in warm seas in the **tropics**, but other kinds of cephalopods live in very cold seas. Some kinds of cephalopods prefer to live on the sea floor all the time and some prefer to live in the open sea all the time. Other kinds of cephalopods live on the sea floor for part of the day and in the open sea at other times of the day.

The sea floor

Most octopuses live on the sea floor. Sometimes they swim near the bottom, but most of the time they crawl over the sea floor. Octopuses crawl about on their arms. They use the suckers on their arms to grip onto hard surfaces and pull their bodies up and over rocks and **corals**.

 This octopus lives under rocks on the sea floor.

Some octopuses live in holes under rocks or corals, or in gaps between the rocks. The hole or space where an octopus lives is called its **den**. Octopuses can squeeze their soft bodies through very small spaces, so the den's opening can be very small.

This tiny octopus has found a drink can to use as a den.

Did you know ?

Some octopuses make their dens in empty seashells or in empty bottles or cans that people throw away.

Some cephalopods hide by burying themselves under sand or mud on the sea floor. They often bury themselves during the day and come out to hunt for food at night.

Some small cephalopods hide between and under plants growing on the sea floor. Some tiny squids are small enough to hide under a leaf of seagrass. The smallest of these squids are less than 1 inch (3 centimeters) long. They make a special glue to stick their bodies to a leaf of seagrass or to seaweed while they rest during the day. At night, they swim over the sea floor and look for food.

Fascinating fact

Different kinds of cephalopods live in different parts of the world. The seas near Australia have a greater variety of cephalopods than anywhere else in the world.

Did you know ?

Some young octopuses and cuttlefishes float and swim near the surface of the sea, but they grow into adults that live on or near the sea floor.

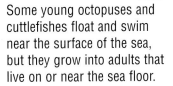 **Some cephalopods hide under sand on the sea floor. This one has left its eyes uncovered so it can look for small animals to catch and eat.**

Some tiny cephalopods hide in patches of seagrass and seaweed.

The open sea

Many cephalopods live in the open sea. They swim using their funnels, but some can swim better than others. Squids and cuttlefishes are very good swimmers and can move very quickly through the water. Their bodies have fins on the sides. These fins help them keep their balance as they glide through the water.

Nautiluses

A nautilus stores gas inside its shell to help it float. During the day, nautiluses float and swim in very deep water. They have a funnel to swim with, but their big shell only lets them swim slowly. Most of the time nautiluses swim backwards. At night, they swim to undersea cliffs, then float and swim next to the cliff to look for food.

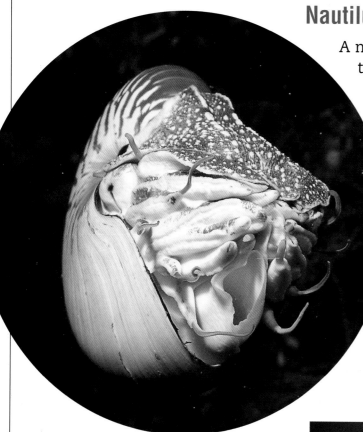

During the day, nautiluses swim in deep water. At night, they swim close to undersea cliffs to look for food.

Squids

Most squids can swim better than other kinds of cephalopods. Some kinds of squids can swim faster than any other invertebrate. Their long, narrow bodies can easily shoot through the water.

Did you know

Some kinds of squids are called flying squids. They swim so fast that they can leap out of the water and glide for a while through the air. Some people have seen these squids accidentally leap onto ships!

Most squids are very good swimmers and live in the open sea.

Cuttlefishes

Cuttlefishes are good swimmers, but they are slower than many kinds of squids. Cuttlefishes often stay close to the sea floor, but some kinds also swim in the open sea. They swim by squirting water through their funnels and by flapping their fins.

Octopuses

Most octopuses live on the sea floor, but some live in the open sea. Some octopuses that live in the open sea never touch the sea floor. Others only swim in the open sea part of the time and live on the sea floor the rest of the time.

Many octopuses swim using their funnels, but some have a different way of swimming. Some octopuses that live in very deep water have webbed arms. To swim, they lift up all their arms at once, then push them down against the water. This movement looks like an umbrella being opened and closed.

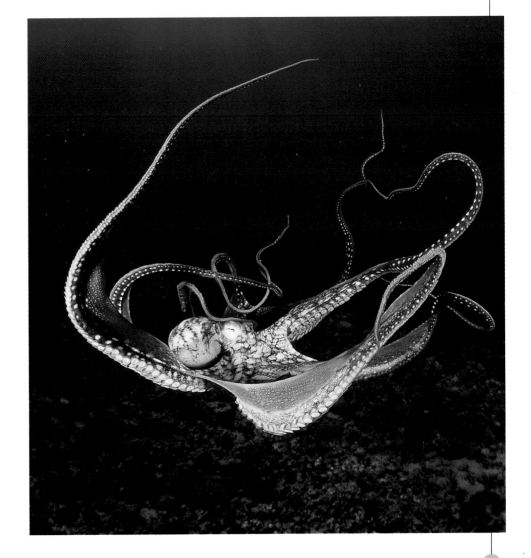

Some octopuses swim in the open sea then sink down to crawl on the sea floor.

Fascinating fact

The large shells of nautiluses and the smaller cuttlebones of cuttlefishes can hold gas inside them. Nautiluses and cuttlefishes use their shells to help them float. They can even change the amount of gas stored inside their shells. If they store more gas inside their shells, they will float closer to the surface of the sea. If they let some gas out of their shells, they will sink closer to the sea floor.

How cephalopods sense the world

Cephalopods have well developed senses to find out about their surroundings. They have large brains to understand all the information that their senses gather. Cephalopods are more intelligent than any other invertebrate.

Light

Most cephalopods have large eyes that are almost the same as human eyes. Eyes sense light. When there is light in their surroundings, cephalopods' eyes can see the shapes and details of objects quite well, but most cannot see colors. Instead, they see how light or dark different objects are. For example, white is seen as being very light, yellow is only a little darker than white, red is darker again and black is very dark.

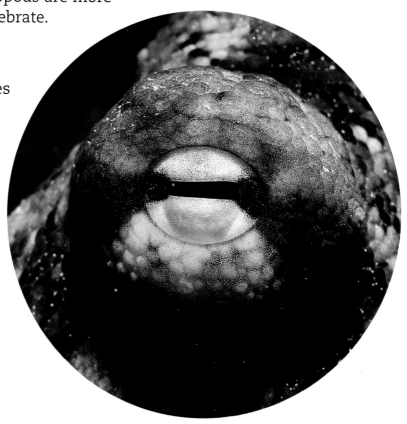

 Most cephalopods, including this octopus, have a large eye on each side of their head.

Did you know

You can explore what it might be like for cephalopods to see objects but not colors. Try looking at a television with the color setting changed to black and white. The pictures show things in black, white and many different shades of gray. You cannot see colors, but you can see if one object is darker or lighter than another one.

Touch

Cephalopods have the sense of touch. They feel their surroundings with their arms and tentacles. Many cephalopods have suckers on their arms or tentacles. The skin on the suckers is very sensitive and can feel things better than other parts of the body.

Smell and taste

Cephalopods can smell and taste chemicals in their surroundings. The skin on the suckers of their arms and tentacles is very good at smelling and tasting things. Cephalopods also smell and taste the water as they swim. When a cephalopod swims, it sucks water inside its body through holes or slits between its head and mantle. It smells and tastes this water with its skin and then squirts the water out its funnel. This helps cephalopods find out which way they should swim to find food.

▽ **Cephalopods use their arms and tentacles to feel, smell and taste things. They also smell and taste the water when they suck it in through the slits between their head and mantle.**

slit where water is sucked into the body

Gravity

Cephalopods can sense **gravity**. A cephalopod uses this sense to find out about the position of its body. It uses this sense to tell if its body is upright or sideways. Without this sense, a cephalopod would not be able to tell if it was moving up, down or straight ahead. This sense also lets a cephalopod know when its body turns or changes position.

Fascinating fact

Octopuses use their tentacles to feel their surroundings, but they cannot figure out the shapes of objects using their sense of touch. They need to see an object to discover its shape.

What cephalopods eat

Cephalopods eat animals. They mostly eat small fishes and crustaceans such as crabs, prawns and shrimps, but they also eat mollusks such as sea snails, mussels and other cephalopods. Many cephalopods are **predators**. A predator is an animal that hunts and kills other animals to eat. Some cephalopods are scavengers that find dead animals to eat.

Did you know ❓

Mollusks, including cephalopods, are the only animals that have radulas.

Cephalopods have a mouth called a beak. The beak has hard jaws like a bird's beak. Cephalopods use their beaks to bite their food into pieces. The pieces of food are then pulled inside the mouth using a special tongue called a radula. The radula is covered with many rows of sharp teeth. It helps cephalopods grind their food into tiny bits they can swallow.

Scavengers

Nautiluses and some other cephalopods are scavengers. Their senses of smell and taste help them find dead animals floating in the water or lying on the sea floor. Nautiluses search for food with their tentacles. Their tentacles find and grab hold of their food while they eat it.

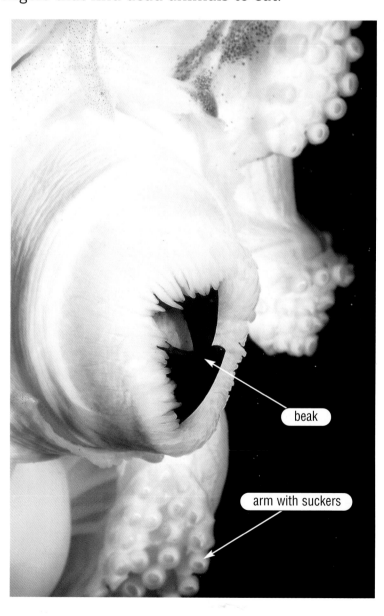

beak

arm with suckers

▷ **This is a cephalopod's beak. The beak is surrounded by arms and tentacles.**

This cuttlefish has caught a fish to eat. It has pulled the fish towards its mouth with its two long feeding tentacles.

Predators

Most cephalopods are predators. When they sense an animal to eat, they are quick to grab it. Octopuses catch their **prey** with their arms, but squids and cuttlefishes catch their prey with their long tentacles. Suckers on the arms and on the ends of the tentacles grip the prey while it is killed and eaten.

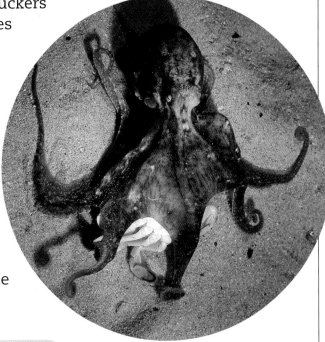

This octopus has caught a crab to eat.

Most octopuses and cuttlefishes have a special way of killing their prey. They bite their prey and inject saliva that has a poison in it. The poison paralyzes the prey, making it easier to kill and eat. Some octopuses use their poison on sea snails and bivalves such as clams or mussels. The octopus drills a small hole through the shell then injects its poison through the hole. The poison makes it easy for the octopus to open the shell and eat the soft body inside.

Did you know

Nautiluses have many tentacles, but their tentacles do not have suckers. Instead, parts of their tentacles are covered with a sticky glue that helps them grip their food.

How do you say it?

radula: *rad-yoo-la*

How cephalopods defend themselves

Many animals like to eat cephalopods. Large cephalopods are eaten by large animals including fishes, sharks, dolphins and whales. Small cephalopods are eaten by fishes, crabs, bigger cephalopods, birds, people and other animals. Cephalopods have many ways to defend themselves from these predators.

Scaring predators

Some cephalopods try to scare predators away by changing their body size, shape and color. Octopuses are good at making their bodies look bigger. A frightened octopus will puff up its body, flatten its arms and change color to look bigger. Some squids, cuttlefishes and octopuses flash different bright colors to scare a predator.

Cephalopods that live on the seashore need to defend themselves from predators that live on land, as well predators that live in the sea. Some octopuses that live on the seashore can scare away birds and other land predators by pointing their funnel at them and squirting them with water.

Fascinating fact

Some octopuses and cuttlefishes have large eye spots. Eye spots are colored patterns on the skin that look like eyes. Large eye spots can make a cephalopod seem much bigger than it really is. A predator can be scared away if it thinks the cephalopod is much bigger than it really is.

Hiding

Hiding on the sea floor

Some octopuses hide by burying themselves under sand. Some octopuses and cuttlefishes hide in dens. Sometimes they block the entrance of their den with rocks, shells or coral.

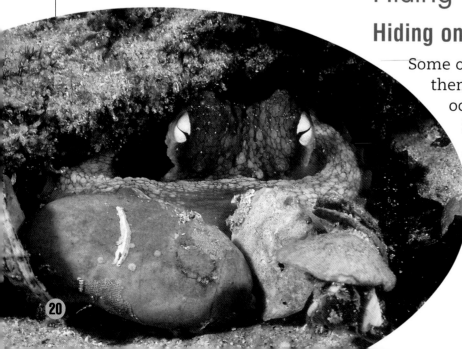

◄ **This octopus is hiding in a den and has partly blocked the entrance with rocks.**

Camouflage

Most cephalopods can **camouflage** their bodies very well. They can change the colors and the patterns on their bodies to match their surroundings. They can make their bodies one color or patterned with different colors. Many cephalopods can only change a few colors. For example, the common cuttlefish can only use dark browns, light browns, grays and white when it changes its body color. These dull colors let it camouflage itself against rocks and sand.

Many cuttlefishes and octopuses can also camouflage their body shape. They push up little flaps or spikes of skin that make them look like seaweeds, rocks or corals.

These two pictures show how an octopus can change the color of its skin.

> **This octopus is not camouflaged here.**

Fascinating fact

A cephalopod's skin contains many tiny dots of color. A cephalopod can change the color of its skin by making some dots smaller and others bigger. For example, if it makes all its color dots shrink, its skin turns white. If it makes all its red dots big, its skin turns red.

> **After only one minute, the octopus has changed its body color to match its surroundings. It is now camouflaged.**

How do you say it?

camouflage: *kam-uh-flaj*

Shells

Nautiluses have a large, strong shell to protect their bodies. When a nautilus needs to defend itself, it will pull its tentacles, head and funnel inside its shell and close the shell's opening with a thick flap called a hood. The main threat to nautiluses is from other cephalopods that drill holes through the nautilus' shells, then poison and eat them. Some people also trap and kill nautiluses so they can sell their beautiful shells.

Escaping

Swimming

Many cuttlefishes, squids and octopuses are good swimmers. This helps them escape many predators. They can swim quickly because they do not have a large shell to slow them down. A cephalopod can swim slowly or quickly depending on how quickly it squirts water out its funnel. Cephalopods swim fastest when they swim backwards.

hood

⊙ **A nautilus can pull its body inside its shell and close the opening with a thick flap called a hood.**

22

Squirting ink

Most cephalopods can squirt out a dark liquid called ink. As soon as it squirts its ink, the cephalopod quickly swims away to escape danger. Sometimes the ink is squirted out in a thick blob that looks a bit like a cephalopod's body. The blob of ink makes a predator think the cephalopod is still there when it has really swum away. Sometimes the ink is squirted out in a wide spray. This cloud of ink hides the cephalopod so predators cannot see it escape.

These two pictures show how an octopus can squirt out ink when it is disturbed.

This picture shows the octopus before it has squirted out ink.

This picture shows the octopus hidden behind its cloud of ink.

Dropping arms

Some octopuses can break arms off their bodies if a predator attacks them. The arm that has been broken off crawls about and flashes different colors to attract the predator's attention. The octopus escapes while the predator is busy eating the arm. The octopus then grows another arm.

Fascinating fact

Many cephalopods that live at the bottom of the sea do not make ink. These cephalopods live where it is always very dark. Ink is not useful in these places because predators cannot see the ink in the dark water.

Blue-ringed

Blue-ringed octopuses are the most dangerous cephalopods in the world. Many octopuses have poison in their saliva that helps them kill their prey. Blue-ringed octopuses have a poison that is so strong it can kill a person!

Blue-ringed octopuses are small octopuses that live for less than one year. They live in shallow water around Australia and parts of Asia. Like other octopuses, blue-ringed octopuses use their poison to kill their prey so they can eat it. They eat crabs, shrimps, small fishes and some mollusks. When a blue-ringed octopus bites its prey, some of its poison is injected into the animal. The poison paralyzes the animal so the octopus can eat it.

This blue-ringed octopus is hunting for prey. Its blue rings can be hard to see when it is not excited or upset.

If a blue-ringed octopus gets excited or is disturbed, it changes color to show its bright blue rings or stripes. There are several different kinds of blue-ringed octopuses. Some blue-ringed octopuses show large blue circles or rings all over their mantle and arms. Some have tiny blue rings all over their mantle and arms. Others have blue lines on their mantle and small blue rings on their arms. These bright blue markings are a warning to predators to stay away.

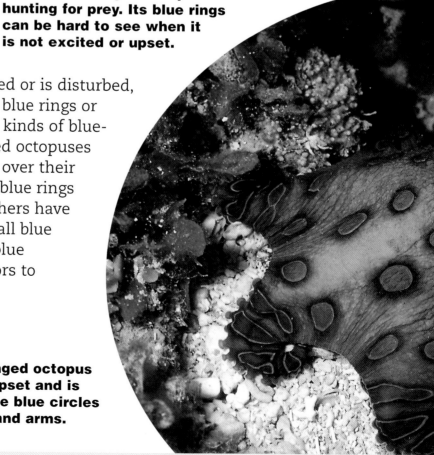

This blue-ringed octopus is excited or upset and is displaying large blue circles on its mantle and arms.

octopuses

If a predator attacks a blue-ringed octopus, the octopus will bite the predator to try to escape. Sometimes people pick up these little octopuses on the seashore. The octopus thinks it is being attacked and defends itself by biting. A person who is injected with poison becomes paralyzed and cannot breathe. The person then needs to be given mouth-to-mouth resuscitation until the poison wears off.

Blue-ringed octopuses do not lay their eggs in a den or on the sea floor. The female holds her eggs in the webbed skin between her arms and carries them until they hatch. A female who is carrying her eggs will sometimes attack and bite an intruder. She does this to protect her eggs so they can hatch safely. When the eggs hatch, the female dies.

⚠ **This blue-ringed octopus is carrying her eggs with her. She is displaying small blue circles on her mantle and arms as a warning to predators to stay away.**

Fascinating fact

Some octopuses have a blue ring on the skin near each eye, but they do not have many blue rings on their bodies like blue-ringed octopuses. When they are frightened, these octopuses puff up their bodies to make the two rings larger and easier to see. These two rings look like very large eyes. The rings are eye spots and are used to scare away predators.

How do you say it?
resuscitation: *ree-suss-i-tay-shon*

A giant cuttlefish

The biggest kind of cuttlefish in the world is the giant cuttlefish of Australia. This cuttlefish can grow as long as 3 feet (1 meter) from the tip of its mantle to the ends of its tentacles. It lives for up to two years. The giant cuttlefish is an expert at changing color. It can show a changing display of bright colors such as red, blue, yellow and green. Then, in less than one second, it can change its color to browns or greens and turn its skin from smooth to spiky so it looks like seaweed.

> **This is a giant cuttlefish.**

A giant octopus

The biggest kind of octopus in the world is the giant Pacific octopus. It can grow more than 16 feet (5 meters) long and live for three to five years. Females lay their eggs in a rocky den on the sea floor. They look after their eggs for about six months until they hatch. The females do not eat while they are looking after their eggs, and they die soon after their eggs hatch. The young octopuses drift in the sea for up to 12 weeks. Then they move to the sea floor to live.

cephalopods

Did you know

Giant squids eat fishes, prawns and other squids. Giant squids are eaten by sperm whales.

A giant squid

The biggest kind of cephalopod is the giant squid. Giant squids are also the largest invertebrates in the world. The longest giant squid ever found was washed up on a beach in New Zealand. Its body was about 59 feet (18 meters) long from the tip of its mantle to the ends of its long tentacles. That is almost as long as two buses! No one has ever seen a living giant squid. The only ones that scientists have been able to see and measure have been found dead. Some have been found washed up on beaches, some have been found inside the stomachs of sperm whales and some have been caught in deep-sea fishing nets.

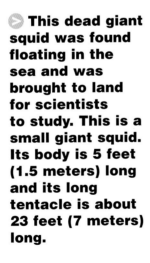

> **This dead giant squid was found floating in the sea and was brought to land for scientists to study. This is a small giant squid. Its body is 5 feet (1.5 meters) long and its long tentacle is about 23 feet (7 meters) long.**

Fascinating fact

A giant squid's eyes are larger than any other animal's eyes. Each eye can grow to about 10 inches (25 centimeters) wide!

Where can you see cephalopods?

The seashore

Octopuses can sometimes be seen on the seashore. The best place to look for them is on rocky seashores that have deep rock pools. The best time to see them is at **low tide** just before sunset. Some octopuses wander about at low tide looking for food. They crawl about in deep rock pools and sometimes they crawl over the rocks to move from one rock pool to another.

If you wander along a sandy beach as the tide goes out, you might find some cuttlebones washed up. Have a close look at them. Can you see any marks on them? These marks might have been made by a predator that ate the cuttlefish's body. Some cuttlebones have teeth marks made by dolphins, seals, sharks or other fishes. Some have marks left by bird's beaks. These can be stab marks made by pointy beaks or cuts such as those made by penguins with biting beaks.

Did you know ?

Octopuses often leave piles of empty seashells and pieces of crab shell outside their dens. These are the remains of their food. If you find a den, an octopus might be nearby, but it will not come out to feed if it sees you.

 These shell-like egg cases sometimes wash up onto beaches. They are made by a kind of octopus called an argonaut. Female argonauts lay their eggs inside the egg cases which float about on the surface of the sea. Sometimes the female argonaut is also washed up inside her egg case.

How do you say it?
argonaut: *ar-go-not*

Safety tips

- Make sure that an adult is nearby when you explore rock pools, rocky shores and other seashores. Rocky shores can be dangerous places to explore because the rocks can be slippery and big waves sometimes crash over the rocks. An adult can watch out for these big waves and help you explore safely.

- If you find an octopus, do not pick it up as it might bite you! Its bite can poison or kill you, especially if it is a blue-ringed octopus.

Fish shops

Many fish shops and fish markets sell squids, octopuses and cuttlefishes that people buy to eat. If you want to have a close look at the body of one of these cephalopods, you can buy a dead one from a fish shop. If you ask for one that has not been cleaned, it will still have its visceral mass and hard mouth.

Lay the cephalopod out with its arms at one end and its mantle and visceral mass at the other end. Look in the middle for the cephalopod's head. Can you see its eyes? Look in the center of all its arms. Can you see and feel its hard mouth? Look for the funnel underneath the head. What other body features can you see? You might like to look inside its body too. If so, get an adult to help you cut the mantle open.

Did you know ?

Some kinds of squids are sold in fish shops and restaurants. They are often called calamari. Calamari rings are slices of the squid's body after the outside skin and the inside visceral mass have been removed.

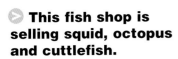
▶ **This fish shop is selling squid, octopus and cuttlefish.**

Quiz

1 Is a cephalopod an invertebrate? Why?

2 What is found in a circle around a cephalopod's mouth?

3 Which of the following kinds of cephalopods have both arms and tentacles?

nautiluses   squids
octopuses   cuttlefishes

4 What does a cephalopod use its funnel for?

5 How many times do most cephalopods reproduce before they die?

6 Where do cephalopods live?

7 Cephalopods have large eyes, but can their eyes see things like our eyes can?

8 What do cephalopods eat?

9 Some cephalopods make ink. What do they use this ink for?

10 What are the most dangerous cephalopods in the world?

Challenge
QUESTIONS

1 How does the shell of a nautilus help it float?

2 How does a cephalopod change the color of its skin?

3 Many cephalopods that live at the bottom of the sea do not make ink. Why?

4 Some cephalopods have colorful patterns on their skin that look like large eyes. What are these used for?

5 Which cephalopods have eyes that are larger than any other animal's eyes?

Turn to page 32 to check your answers.

Divers sometimes find cuttlefishes near the sea floor.

Glossary

camouflage Colors, patterns and ways of covering an animal's body that make the animal hard to see against its background.

corals Tiny invertebrate animals that live in large groups and make coral reefs.

den A hole under rocks or corals or in small gaps between rocks where some octopuses and cuttlefishes live.

foot The strong, flat muscle that mollusks such as snails use to crawl.

funnel A strong, tube-shaped muscle found under a cephalopod's body. A cephalopod swims by squirting a jet of water through its funnel to push its body along.

gravity The power of Earth to pull things downwards. For example, if you jump up off the ground, gravity pulls you back down.

low tide When the sea goes out and leaves more of the seashore uncovered than at high tide.

mantle A special part of the skin on the top of a mollusk's body that grows its shell. A cephalopod has a thick mantle that covers most of its body.

mollusks A group of invertebrate animals that includes snails, slugs, chitons, bivalves and cephalopods. A mollusk has a soft body, a mantle and either a strong foot or a funnel.

predators Animals that hunt other animals to eat.

prey Animals that are eaten by other animals.

reproduce To make more of the same kind of animal or plant.

sperm Cells from a male animal's body that can fertilize the eggs from a female animal's body to reproduce.

tentacles Special body parts that many cephalopods use to capture their food. Tentacles are very long and thin with either a few suckers at the ends or no suckers at all. They can bend and can often be made longer or shorter.

tropics The part of the Earth between the Tropic of Cancer and the Tropic of Capricorn, where air and water temperatures are always warm or hot.

visceral mass The part of a mollusk's body that contains its stomach, heart and other body organs.

Index

A
arms 5, 6, 7, 9, 10, 11, 12, 15, 16, 17, 19, 23

C
camouflage 21
color 9, 20, 21, 24, 26
cuttlebones 8, 15, 28

D
den 12, 20, 25, 26, 28

E
eyes 6, 16, 20, 25, 27
eye spots 20, 25

F
food 7, 13, 14, 17, 18, 28
funnel 5, 6, 7, 8, 14, 15, 17, 20, 22

I
ink 23
invertebrate 4, 5, 14, 16, 27

M
mantle 5, 6, 7, 8, 17, 24, 25
mollusks 5, 18, 24

P
poison 19, 22, 24, 25, 29
predators 18, 19, 20, 21, 22, 23, 24, 25
prey 19, 24

R
radula 18

S
scavengers 18
shell 5, 6, 7, 8, 14, 15, 19, 22
suckers 6, 7, 9, 12, 16, 17, 18, 19

T
tentacles 5, 6, 7, 9, 10, 16, 17, 18, 19

V
visceral mass 6, 29

Answers to quiz

1 Yes, because a cephalopod is an animal that does not have a backbone.
2 Arms and tentacles.
3 Squids and cuttlefishes.
4 To swim.
5 Only once.
6 Cephalopods live in all parts of the sea.
7 Cephalopods' eyes can see shapes and details like our eyes can, but most cannot see colors.
8 Cephalopods eat animals such as fishes, crabs, prawns, shrimps, sea snails, mussels and other cephalopods.
9 Cephalopods squirt ink out of their bodies to help them escape from predators.
10 Blue-ringed octopuses.

Answers to challenge questions

1 A nautilus can store gas inside its shell to help it float. It floats closer to the surface if it puts more gas inside its shell. It sinks deeper in the water if it lets gas out of its shell.
2 A cephalopod's skin contains many tiny dots of color. It can change its color by making some color dots bigger and others smaller.
3 It is dark at the bottom of the sea and the ink is of no use because predators cannot see it.
4 These large eye spots can scare predators away. Predators see the eye spots and think that the cephalopod is a much bigger animal than it really is.
5 Giant squids (their eyes can grow about 10 inches (25 centimeters) wide).